Model of the Pergamon Acropolis
(cf. fig. 10, p. 15)

1 Storage magazines
2 Palace I
3 Palace III
4 Palace IV
5 Palace V
6 Gate
7 Temple sanctuary of Athena
8 Trajaneum (temple built by the Roman emperor Trajan)
9 Library
10 Theater of Dionysus
11 Temple of Dionysus
12 The Pergamon Altar
13 Upper Agora (marketplace)
14 Heroon (building for the celebration of the cult of the local rulers)

The Pergamon Altar

Its Rediscovery
History and Reconstruction

Max Kunze

Staatliche Museen zu Berlin
Preußischer Kulturbesitz
Antikensammlung

48 pages with 26 color, 13 black-and-white illustrations

Photos: Jürgen Liepe (with the exception of figs. 1, 2, 3, 5, 6, 14, 15, 18, 37 and endpapers)
Translation: Biri Fay

Front cover: North projecting hall of the Pergamon Altar
Endpapers: Model of the Pergamon Acropolis
Frontispiece: Artemis's hunting dog bites a giant in the neck
Back cover: Detail of the Eastern Frieze: Porphyrion (cf. fig. 21)

THE REDISCOVERY AND EXCAVATION

"At Pergamon is a great marble altar, 40 feet high, with remarkable statues, and the entire is surrounded by a Battle of the Giants" — *Pergamo ara marmorea magna, alta pedes quadraginta cum maximis sculpturis; continet autem gigantomachiam.* With these words Lucius Ampelius, a Roman, described the Great Altar at Pergamon in his "Book of Memorable Facts" (liber memorialis 8,14). As Ampelius wrote these words the altar was already about 400 years old. Just a few centuries later, however, nothing remained of this extraordinary building. Even so, after the Middle Ages, the odd traveller who included Pergamon in his itinerary was duly impressed by the ancient ruins of the upper and lower city.

As far as we know it was an 18th century Frenchman, Count Marie Gabriel A. F. Choiseul-Gouffier, who first suggested that it might be interesting to excavate the citadel at Pergamon. Another century passed, however, before a systematic excavation was finally underway.

Although a few fragments of Pergamene relief had been sent to the Berlin Museums in 1871, once there they had gone virtually unnoticed. It was Alexander Conze, archaeologist and director of the Sculpture Collection of the Royal Berlin Museums, who was finally attracted to the three relief fragments which were described at the time as hanging "on the wall close to the floor in the so-called Hall of Heroes in the Old Museum". At last the significance of the fragments had been recognized and the connection between Ampelius's description of a great altar decorated with a battle of the giants and the representations on the relief fragments in Berlin emerged.

The man who had discovered the reliefs and sent them to Berlin was a German engineer named Carl Humann (fig. 1) who was working for road construction firms in Turkey at the time. In his opinion, the reliefs depicted a "battle with men, horses, wild animals" that had been created for a Temple of Minerva at Pergamon. It was clear to the Berliners, however, that the relief fragments were from a Gigantomachy, or battle of the gods and the giants. Furthermore, they were convinced that it was the Gigantomachy encircling The Pergamon Altar seen by Ampelius centuries earlier.

Alexander Conze immediately sent word to Humann that he should watch out for more reliefs. September 1878 — barely a year had passed and the Berlin Museums, officially licensed by the Turkish state authorities, began to excavate the Pergamon citadel. Carl Humann, the man who rediscovered Pergamon was appointed excavation site director.

Fig. 1
Carl Humann in Smyrna (Archives DAI Istanbul)

Going back a few years in Pergamon's modern history to the winter of 1864/65, we find Carl Humann arriving at Pergamon for the first time. He was attracted by the idea of visiting the once thriving city of the fabled Kings of Pergamon. In his report he wrote, "Then it was up to citadel. To the casual observer it looks like one big field of rubble covered with grass and low bushes interspersed with projecting walls from various periods and whose relationship to each other is not at first glance clear; the crown of the citadel includes what is apparently a Turkish wall which acted as fortification before the hill fell into its present desolate state. Here too, at the summit, a massive foundation, often criss-crossing and spreading in all directions, projects from the ground. Especially of note, however, bordering the precipice to the east as the west,

Fig. 2
The exposed foundations of The Pergamon Altar (Photograph courtesy of the Museum)

Fig. 3
Reconstruction of The Pergamon Altar in the old Pergamon Museum in Berlin — 1901—1908 (Photograph: W. Titzenthaler, Berlin)

the high retaining walls of the Attalid period still stand. Not a single block has been displaced over the centuries. Above the western retaining wall I stepped onto the mound of ruins that had been called the Temple of Athena Polias. Sadly I stood there contemplating the magnificent Corinthian capitals almost the height of a man, the many bases and other architectural elements, all scattered and grown over with bushes and wild figs; nearby smoked the limestone oven into which every block of marble entered in small pieces after falling to the blow of the heavy hammer. A few recently dug trenches revealed just how much rubble lay under the wasted ground surface; the

smaller they were smashed, the more convenient they were for the workmen. This, then, was what remained of the proud, invincible seat of the Attalid rulers".

After his first visit Humann did his best to protect the antiquities to the point that he even temporarily moved his residence to Pergamon. He knew, however, that only an excavation could really offer satisfactory protection by safeguarding the entire area. His hopes of winning the Berlin Museums for such an excavation appeared to materialize in 1871. In that year a group of Berlin architectural researchers and archaeologists travelling in Turkey accepted his invitation to visit Pergamon. This gave

Fig. 5
The Byzantine wall where the first reliefs were found by Carl Humann
Drawing by Christian Wilberg (Photograph courtesy of the Museum)

him the chance to show them the boldly carved reliefs he had found built into the Byzantine wall. At the end of the same year he sent those first reliefs to Berlin. To understand why it still took years before things actually got going at Pergamon, we must consider the contemporary historical and cultural situation.

◁ *Fig. 4*
The west side of The Pergamon Altar today

Thanks to Prussia's military success, the German Empire had been proclaimed in 1871. Understandably the new imperial capital of Berlin called upon its research institutions and museums to help establish a worthy cultural legitimacy. In a letter to the king, the Prussian Minister of Culture bluntly stated the situation, "It is of particular importance that the collections of the museums, thus far very weak in original works of Greek art . . ., acquire a work of Greek art that only the numerous Attic and Near Eastern sculptures in The British Museum can compare to or approach".

In 1875 the Berlin archaeologist, Ernst Curtius, actualized a dream that had been nurtured by German archaeologists for decades — he initiated excavations at the sacred precinct of Olympia. The excavations, however, were subject to the strict Greek antiquities laws and therefore yielded scant dividends for the museum collections. The antiquities laws stated that only "duplicates" of finds were permitted

to leave Greece for Berlin. Understandably disappointed, the officials in charge, including Bismarck, temporarily blocked the funding earmarked for the excavation at Olympia.

At the time the Berlin Museums were "being reorganized with an eye toward successful undertakings" and in the process were being drawn closer than ever to the Ministries of Culture and Education. The Ministries felt that in order to bring the Berlin Museums up to par with the collections in The Louvre and The British Museum, excavations should be undertaken in Turkey where the chances to expand the collections seemed better.

Numerous uprisings against the Turks as well as the war between Turkey and Russia had worked in favor of the young German Empire by increasing its influence with the Ottoman Empire. Permission to excavate at Pergamon was obtained easily. The division of finds originally agreed upon between Turkey and Berlin was renegotiated with

Fig. 6
View of The Pergamon Altar during the excavation of 1879 Drawing by Christian Wilberg (Photograph courtesy of the Museum)

Fig. 7   ▷
Over life-sized female statues which were found near The Pergamon Altar
Antikensammlung Berlin

Fig. 8   ▷▷
Portrait of King Attalos I(?) (241—197 BC)
Antikensammlung Berlin

11

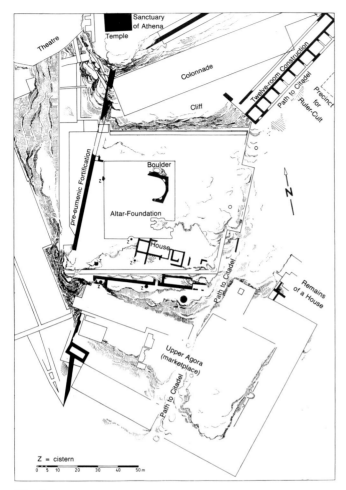

Fig. 9
Plan of the terrace below the Temple of Athena with fore-runners of The Pergamon Altar

friend of Humann did not exist, and we could not know then, what has become possible with his help, that the remaining ruins could be protected from the stone robbers of the modern city. . . ."

On the 9th of September, 1878, Carl Humann began the search for the famous altar on the Acropolis of Pergamon. Clearly, the goal of the first excavation campaign was to find the rest of the magnificent reliefs which were artistically the most important part of the ancient monument. Thanks to Carl Humann and Alexander Conze (who offered his valuable advice and suggestions first from Berlin and from 1879 onward, at the site itself), the excavation was never quite reduced to a treasure hunt despite excavation methods clearly aimed at quick results.

Humann began his work on the Byzantine city wall that once protected the Acropolis (fig. 5). A number of years earlier he had discovered the first fragmentary relief panels built into the southern wall at this spot. Within a very few days his results were impressive and by the end of September twenty-three panels from the Gigantomachy had been discovered. Humann continued his exploration to the north of the site and there too met with success. Not only did he uncover remains of the altar's original foundation (fig. 6), but he also discovered that when the altar was torn down during the Byzantine period, many of its elements had been used to build a retaining wall. Furthermore, he discovered that parts of the eastern frieze must have been used to construct a number of small buildings on the altar's former terrace. Near the altar's dense foundation, he found the important Zeus and Athena group. Humann wrote with great enthusiasm in the report covering the first excavation campaign, ". . . the more I consider the finds, the more excited I become. We've found an entire artistic epoch, the largest work preserved from antiquity is right in our hands".

Indeed, as the reliefs rapidly came to light their high artistic quality and the projected length of 120 meters of the reconstructed frieze promised to make the Pergamon frieze, next to The British Museum's Parthenon frieze, the longest and finest preserved from ancient Greece. Tradition has it that when the Athena group was freed from its blanket of earth someone exclaimed, "Now we have a Laokoon too". This was in all likelihood less a recognition of the similarity between Athena's opponent, Alkyoneus, and the famous Laokoon in the Belvedere in Rome, than it was an unconscious observation of the powerful expressive quality and the high artistic level shared by both works, characteristics of the Pergamene school (fig. 17, 18). Since that time the truth of this spontaneous observation has became clear. Recently, it has been argued convincingly that Pergamene sculptors created the original of Rome's

Bismarck's support in 1878–1879. The new agreement stated that in exchange for 20,000 Marks, the Turkish government would permit all finds relating to The Pergamon Altar to go to Berlin. Later, reminiscing over the departure of the Pergamon finds for Berlin, Alexander Conze wrote, "We are not totally indifferent to the implications of uprooting the remains of a great monument from its native soil to bring it to us where we will not ever again be able to offer it the light and surroundings in which it was created, and in which it once was fully effective. Yet we have seized it from certain, complete destruction. In those days a Hamdy Bey who was soon to become a close

Laokoon at about the same time The Pergamon Altar itself was being built.

Although the transport of the altar finds was just beginning in 1879, Humann and Conze were already making a few speculative sketches for its reconstruction. In addition to the foundation measurements, the corner panels of the Great Frieze offered orientation points for a reconstruction. The missing link, however, was first found in the spring of 1883: the length of the friezes at the sides of the great stairway. Finally it was possible to determine the width of the stairway and the sequence of the frieze panels. Another five years of intensive analysis were necessary, however, before the Berlin archaeologists and architectural specialists, Otto Puchstein and Richard Bohn, were satisfied with the relationship and order of the frieze panels as well as the architectural composition of the altar itself. Among other things, during the reconstruction in Berlin, they discovered placement marks in the form of sequence letters carved in the ledge above the frieze which also bore the names of the gods. The deciphering of this ancient code made it possible to order the ledge blocks and, with the names of the gods now in the correct order, establish the sequence of the relief panels.

Carl Humann's work at Pergamon, and the reconstruction of the altar in Berlin by two Italian sculptors recruited for the job, went amazingly quickly. In April 1880, after six months' work, Humann noted in the excavation statistics that 97 relief panels of the Gigantomachy and 2000 fragments (about three-fifths of the entire length), 35 panels from the Telephus frieze and 100 fragments, as well as numerous free-standing statues, busts, inscriptions and architectural elements had been excavated.

The speed at which Humann worked was admittedly at the expense of centuries of accumulated settlement levels. These later levels of civilization, late antique, Byzantine and Arabic, were unfortunately removed without being properly examined or documented. Only Imperial and Roman architectural elements were deemed important.

By the end of the first excavation campaign in April 1880, Alexander Conze had set his sights beyond the altar terrace. In Berlin he stressed the need for additional funding to excavate the upper part of the imperial city. His pleas were answered and during the two following excavation campaigns — August 1880 to December 1881 and April 1883 to December 1886 — Carl Humann examined the remaining monuments on the Acropolis of Pergamon with the valuable assistance of experienced architects. The Terrace of Athena was investigated and the Temple of Trajan, the Royal Palace and the Theater of Dionysus followed suit.

By the time the excavation closed on the 15th of December, 1886, the entire upper city as well as sections of the lower

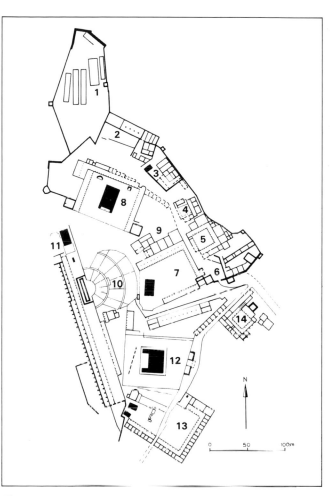

Fig. 10
Plan of the Pergamon Acropolis

1   Storage magazines
2—5 Palaces
6   Gate
7   Temple sanctuary of Athena
8   Trajaneum (temple built by the Roman emperor Trajan)
9   Library
10 Theater of Dionysus
11 Temple of Dionysus
12 The Pergamon Altar
13 Upper Agora (marketplace)
14 Heroon (building for the celebration of the cult of the local rulers)

15

city had been explored. Even the subterranean water conduit, which by means of pressure had supplied the ancient city with water from the north, had been thoroughly investigated.

For many contemporaries, the discovery of Pergamon's High Hellenistic art was just as exciting as Heinrich Schliemann's controversial excavations, since 1871, underway at Troy. Thanks to a cleverly planned publicity program, Schliemann's discoveries were certainly more in the headlines. The finds at Pergamon, however, produced a far stronger cultural and artistic wave. The initial shock from the Pergamene artistic style, characterized by remarkably realistic detail, dynamic movement and rich compositional tension, was reflected in the words of a renowned contemporary archaeologist. He called it "superficial naturalism" and a "vile outrage of Hellenistic art". With the discovery of this Late Hellenistic style, a new chapter in the history of Greek art had been opened.

The Pergamon Altar was reconstructed in the Altes Museum in the center of Berlin. Thanks in part to the contemporary artistic taste, the initial visitor reaction to the monument, articles in newspapers and journals and its reception by artists and writers were equally enthusiastic. Clearly the Wilhelminian preference for the baroque made the High Hellenistic Pergamene style particularly popular. In the words of one admirer, "something related to our modern thought and perception" could be discovered in this ancient art. Others immediately saw the affinity to the contemporary political situation. To its admirers, Pergamon had been an "ambitious center of power and culture where one had had the means to attract the finest craftsmen". Its splendid altar was seen as the "proudest monument of monarchist self-confidence", a role which it was also to fill in Berlin. The fledgling German empire had adopted The Pergamon Altar and its symbolic meaning, which whether ancient or modern, was practically identical. The historical parallels were close at hand. Just as the Hellenistic Empire of Pergamon superseded the Classical city culture of Athens, so were the small states of Germany swallowed into the empire under Prussia's leadership.

Fig. 11
Statue of Athena Parthenos from the Library at Pergamon
Antikensammlung Berlin

REPRESENTATION AND CULT

THE ACROPOLIS OF PERGAMON UNDER THE ATTALIDS

The Great Altar of Pergamon was built on a large terrace near the summit of the Acropolis. As the city was already some years old when the altar was built, a number of older buildings were first razed (fig. 9). In addition, the terrace was enlarged with the help of substructures and similar to a Greek temple, a separate enclosure was created. The street, which in ancient times led over the citadel hill, and through the upper market place to the gate of the citadel, now passed to the east of the altar's sacred precinct (fig. 10). The ancient visitor might have entered the altar precinct through a simple entrance in the enclosure wall, or have continued further up the hill to the temple sanctuary built for Athena (fig. 14), the goddess sacred to the city. The Temple of Athena was about a hundred years older than the Great Altar, probably built before the Attalid Kings ruled Pergamon.

In Greek sacred architecture the temple and the altar were traditionally closely related. At Pergamon, however, the Temple of Athena is higher on the Acropolis than the Great Altar and both buildings are set on their own terraces. But a glance at a plan of the two monuments shows that the connection between their axes was carefully planned. The long side of the temple is aligned with the west side of the altar with its great stairway. When standing in the altar precinct, one could look up and see the far smaller Temple of Athena despite the hill's cliff. By orienting the monumental columned altar at Pergamon to the west, King Eumenes II (197−159 BC) followed the example of earlier altars and heeded traditional cultic rules.

To call this remarkable building an altar, however, is clearly an understatement. The actual altar for burnt offerings was set in a court surrounded by a long, graceful colonnade. Together, the altar for burnt offerings and the colonnade structure were raised on a massive podium which was cut on the west side by a broad flight of twenty-four stairs. The visitor mounted these steep steps to reach the actual altar. The sides of the podium were covered with a frieze 2.30 meter high worked in bold relief depicting the struggle between the gods and the giants.

At Pergamon, the traditional Greek altar had evolved into a construction of monumental proportions; the altar had become a fully independent monument. This architectural concept was not entirely new. It reflected the influence of the architecture of Ionia and Asia Minor where, during the sixth century BC, altars surrounded by horseshoe-shaped

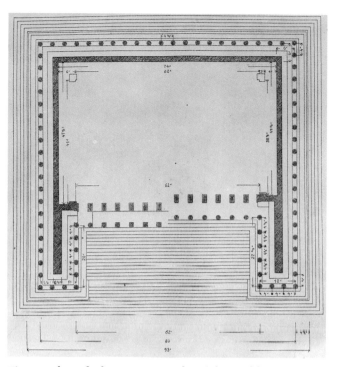

Fig. 12 Plan of The Pergamon Altar (after Kähler)

Fig. 13 The altar of Asklepios at Kos

walls and free standing altars with elevated stairs or walls surrounding an altar court were built.

Although we know a great deal about The Pergamon Altar, there are, nevertheless, many unsolved questions. One of the most difficult is the identification of the deity to whom the temple was dedicated. Could it have been dedicated to the goddess Athena as the archaeological remains suggest? Or was it dedicated to Athena and Zeus together as a number of dedicatory inscriptions on statues found in the course of excavation might seem to indicate? Unfortunately, only a handful of fragments with dedicatory inscriptions were found and these are so inconclusive that they really do not satisfactorily answer the question.

The other major question is the date of the altar's construction. We know that the altar was begun during the reign of King Eumenes II (197–159 BC) of Pergamon. It is also thought that around 180 BC Eumenes II erected other buildings on the Acropolis of Pergamon, for example, the pair of colonnades for the Sanctuary of Athena and its Propylon.

When Rome withdrew its support from the Pergamene kings in 166 BC, it had seriously threatened the stability of the Pergamene empire. Lead by King Eumenes II from 168 to 165 BC, the glorious victories over the Gallian tribes and neighboring enemy empires were so important that the erection of a commemorative monument would have been warranted.

This leads to another question concerning the altar — was it ever finished? We know that King Prusias II of Bithynia invaded Pergamon in 156 BC, destroying large parts of the city and occupying others. In order to rebuild the houses and temples in the lower part of the city, the entire Pergamene work force would have been needed. It may have been at this point that work on The Pergamon Altar came to a standstill.

The Pergamon Altar and the Temple of Athena were only two of the remarkable buildings the ancient visitor might have seen if his travels took him to the Pergamon Acropolis (fig. 10). He might also have visited the impressive two storey high colonnade which had been added to the Temple of Athena to house the art collection begun by Attalos I.

◁ Fig. 14
Entrance to the Temple of Athena at Pergamon
Reconstruction in The Pergamon Museum (Photograph courtesy of the Museum)

In its adjacent rooms a vast library was installed; with around 200,000 scrolls it was, at the time, second only to Alexandria.

A theater dedicated to Dionysus built on the steep, western slope of the Acropolis could hold an audience of 10,000. The theater was entered over a terrace which was supported by a massive substructure and flanked on both sides by colonnades. Over the north end of the terrace rose the temple dedicated to the god Dionysus. The royal palaces in the upper city, as well as the Heroon east of the altar where the cult of the local rulers was practiced, reflect the young Attalid Empire's underlying need to manifest its importance through culture and art.

THE ATTALIDS

A Glorious Era in the History of Pergamon

The majority of the monuments found on the Pergamon Acropolis were erected under the ambitious and enthusiastic patronage of the Attalid kings, Attalos I and Eumenes II.

Pergamon's short but glorious history spans barely 150 years. It begins under a local governor, Philetairos (283–263 BC), who confiscated the treasury which he administered for Seleukos I of Syria following the latter's victory, at Kurupedion, over Lysimachos, King of Thrace as well as the city, the fortress and the entire central Caicus Valley. With this single act, Philetairos laid the foundation for the might of the Attalids which held until 133 BC when the last king of Pergamon, Attalos III, died. In his political testament, King Attalos III left the kingdom of Pergamon to the Romans as *ager publicus*, state land. A few years later Pergamon was made the capital of the Roman province of Asia. Pergamon's ascension to a position of political importance in Asia Minor coincides with the premature

Fig. 15
A Gaul killing his wife and himself
A Roman marble copy after a Pergamene bronze original
Museo Nazionale delle Terme, Rome (Photograph: DAI Rome)

Anatolian peninsula. The astute kings of Pergamon understood quite well the long range advantage of linking themselves to Roman political power and how to take advantage of this link.

The power of the Hellenistic Attalid kings was based on a special social-economic system. The king owned the natural resources which meant that the gold and silver mines as well as the large imperial workshops were royal property. Dependent day workers, mostly native Lydians guarded by royal slaves, worked in the king's workshops. The king also owned the land, the Chora of Pergamon. Farming was carried on by dependent farmers (serfs), and according to oriental custom, the kings of Pergamon had the right to attach land and villages to temples, or bestow them on dignitaries, mostly members of the Macedonian nobility. Here the contrast to the Greek city states is obvious, especially where the land was distributed to free citizens. Yet the tax revenues from the conquered provinces of Pergamon were the Attalids' main financial source for underwriting the ambitious expansion of the cultural metropolis and supporting other cities.

Pergamon's influence also extended to Greek settlements where the ownership relationship remained essentially intact and with it the use of slave labor for private property. The co-existence of two different socio-economic sytems within Pergamon's realm initially encouraged a flourishing economy and the growth of a powerful territorial state.

The rulers of Pergamon, indulged and encouraged by Rome, successfully dealt with the Galatians in the interior of Asia Minor while at the same time bringing other territories under their rule. Pergamon was soon the strongest military and economic power in Asia Minor, and because an important harbor, the coastal city of Ephesos, was at its disposal, Pergamon also ranked as a maritime power to be reckoned with.

Thanks to this excellent socio-economic system the royal house of Pergamon had more than adequate financial means with which to develop their splendid city. Attention was of course centered on the Acropolis whose terraced terrain was gradually developed into an impressive grouping of cult and official buildings. The finest architects and artists were brought to Pergamon where all that they built or created was intended to demonstrate how firmly the artistic heritage of their royal employers was rooted in Greek culture. In effect they were creating a "new Athens", a new center for Greek art, literature and science most visibly expressed in its buildings and works of art.

In 241 BC Attalos I became the ruler of Pergamon and assumed the title of king. After he had successfully brought the Gauls under control, he erected a number of commemorative monuments, the most famous of which

death of Alexander the Great in 323 BC and the fall of his global empire. His successors, the Diadochi, created new divisions to administrate the empire.

Pergamon, once a dependent city in Asia Minor situated 28 kilometers from the coast of the Aegean Sea, developed into a territorial city of impressive dimensions. Its clever rulers and its geographical situation between two large centers of Hellenistic power, the empires of the Antigonids in Macedonia and the Seleucids to the east in Syria, fostered Pergamon's development. Taking advantage of this buffer zone, Pergamon built a strong territorial state on the was built on the citadel in the middle of the Sanctuary of Athena. Although almost nothing of the ancient monument survives, Roman marble copies of some of the original sculptures have been preserved. The best known are the "Dying Gaul" in the Museo Capitolino and "Gaul Killing Himself" in the Museo Nazionale (fig. 15), both in Rome. Through monuments like these which dramatically portray the underdog, the victorious kings of Pergamon successfully practiced their policy of self-enhancement.

In a similar manner, when King Eumenes II (Attalos I's son and successor) erected The Pergamon Altar he used the theme of the Great Frieze, the battle of the giants with the Olympian gods, to symbolize his victories against the Gauls and other neighboring kingdoms. Using the myth as a vehicle, the victories were elevated beyond day to day political and military lore.

Pergamon became a center of Greek culture under the Attalid kings. Greek architects were responsible for important architectural achievements and the artists gathered to work for the kings of Pergamon created works of art that count among the finest of the High Hellenistic period. But Pergamon's cultural policy did not end here. Not only had Pergamon set about becoming the new cultural and scientific center of the Greek world, but also the successor and legitimate heir of fifth and fourth century Greek culture which at that time was considered the Classical age. In arts and politics this aim encouraged a revival of the golden age of Classical Athens. Municipal authorities were elected in order to give the appearance of democracy even though municipal affairs were in actuality determined by five strategists hired by the king.

The heritage of Classical Greece was consciously reflected in architecture and the fine arts. Therefore, it does not come as a surprise that the kings of Pergamon built large colonnades, the stoa of Attalos and the stoa of Eumenes, at the foot of the Athenian Acropolis or gave votive offerings to famous pan-Hellenic sanctuaries in Delphi and Olympia.

A "miniature" copy of Athena Parthenos (fig. 11), the famous gold and ivory cult image created by Phidias for the temple on the Athenian Acropolis, stood in the Library at Pergamon.

The collecting of original works of art and the copying of Archaic and Classical sculpture begun by Attalos I is completely in keeping with the Pergamon kings' interest in the past and their revival of its cultural achievements. Their claim to be the true heirs and champions of Athenian greatness was of course reinforced by victories in Asia Minor as well as those against the Gauls. The kings of Pergamon emerged politically stabilized as "saviors of the Greek cities".

ARA MARMOREA MAGNA

THE GREAT MARBLE ALTAR

When we stand before the full scale reconstruction of The Pergamon Altar on Berlin's Museum Island, we get a very good idea of the grandeur and scale of the original building. Its original massive platform was almost square, 36.44 meters wide and 34.20 meters deep. In the reconstruction, five steps rising from the platform support a monumental pedestal consisting of a base whose sides are covered by a 2.30 meter high frieze of relief panels crowned by a great projecting cornice. The monumental, sculptured frieze is 120 meters long and encircles the entire altar. On the west side the frieze is interrupted by a 20 meter wide flight of stairs which rises against the building and leads to a magnificent colonnade; behind the colonnade where an altar for burnt offerings stood in an open court. The frieze continues at the sides of the grand stairway, narrowing as the steps mount. Here, at the sides of the steps, we discover one of those details that make The Pergamon Altar so interesting. The stairway has been worked right into the composition of the frieze (fig. 28); the gods and the giants literally stand, kneel and lie on the steps.

The colonnade which rises above the frieze is shallow. Its columns are delicate with profiled bases and Ionic capitals which support a richly ornamented entablature. The majority of the water spouts on the gutter ledges were left unfinished and it is possible to see the unworked areas at irregular intervals. Originally the roof was decorated with teams of horses, quadrigas, lion-griffins, centaurs and figures of gods.

Undoubtedly only the select few (priests, members of the royal house and foreign emissaries) were permitted to mount the great stairway during cult festivals, or to pass through the colonnade and enter the open court and approach the altar for burnt offerings. The Ionic columns at the front facing the stairway stand on square bases, while the double Ionic columns facing the court stand on pillar-like rectangular bases. The space between the columns of this west colonnade is greater than elsewhere which makes the colonnade appear lighter. A wall surrounds the court of the altar on three sides where a frieze set at eye level told the life story of Telephus, Pergamon's founder.

The Great Frieze, in a series of dramatic scenes, relates the mythical battle between the gods and the giants which was only won through the intervention of the hero Herakles. The small frieze in the altar court is composed of episodes from the life of Telephus, Herakles's son and founder of the city of Pergamon. The roof of the altar was decorated with

Fig. 16

EASTERN FRIEZE

Demeter, the earth fertility goddess, was probably depicted to the left of the wing fragment of a giant

The triple-bodied Titan, Hekate, goddess of ways, witchcraft and magic is accompanied by her Molossian dog as she fights with torch, sword and lance against Klytios who hurls a boulder

The glance of the bow and arrow armed goddess of the hunt, Artemis, is directed at a naked armed giant who may be Otos. Between the pair, Artemis's hunting dog bites another giant in the neck to death

Leto, by Zeus the mother of Apollo and Artemis, subdues a giant with animal features with her flaming torch

Apollo, the god of medicine and prophecy who wards off evil has struck down the giant, Ephialtes, with his arrow

SOUTHERN FRIEZE

Rhea/Cybele, the great mother goddess from Asia Minor, mounted on a lion and armed with bow and arrow, enters the fray. At the upper left is Zeus's eagle with a bundle of thunderbolts

Three gods who have not yet been identified fight a powerful, bull-necked giant. At the left, in front of a goddess, a god swings his weapon over his head. At the right a kneeling god jabs a weapon into the breast of a giant

Eos, the goddess of the dawn and the leader of the gods of the light, reins in her horse, and with her right hand hurls a torch

Helios, the god of the sun, rises from the sea in his quadriga. One giant places himself before the quadriga, a second is being run over

NORTHERN PROJECTING HALL BESIDE THE GREAT STAIRWAY

The sea god, Triton, Poseidon's son, with his mother, Amphitrite, fights against the giants. Triton has been given a human upper torso with wings, the body of a fish and the front legs of a horse

To the clan of the sea gods belong the pair Nereus, at the right, and Doris followed by Okeanos and, partially preserved, Tethys

NORTHERN FRIEZE

The goddess of love, Aphrodite, pulls a lance from her dead opponent. Her mother, Dione, fights against a winged giant who at the same time is being attacked by Aphrodite's son, Eros

The fighters here are perhaps the Dioscuri, Zeus' twin sons. Polydeuces rushes to Castor's assistance who has been attacked by a giant from behind who crushes him in his arms and bites into his upper arm

Also accompanying the war god are the three following groups of fighters: at the left, a god pulls out a tree to use as a weapon; in the middle, a winged goddess drives a spear into the breast of her opponent; at the right, a god struggles with a giant wearing chest armor

Hera, Zeus' wife, drives the quadriga. The winged horses were associated with the four winds, Notos, Boreas, Zephyros and Euros

According to the myth, Herakles was responsible for the victory of the gods. Only the inscription and the paws from his lion skin today mark the place where he once fought

Zeus, the most important of the Olympians who collected the clouds, sent the rain and threw thunderbolts, accompanied by an eagle fights the leader of the giants, Porphyrion, and two young giants

Athena, the daughter of Zeus and goddess of the city, separates the giant, Alkyoneus, from his mother, Gaia, who is buried to her waist in her earthly domain. At the upper right, the winged goddess of victory, Nike, approaches

The god of war, Ares, with his team of horses who rear up before a winged giant

Theia, the mother of the morning and the evening star, appears here with her children Eos, Helios and Selene

Selene, the moon goddess who hides the day, is shown from the back galloping over a giant on her mule

A young god, perhaps Aither, strangles a giant with serpent legs, human body, lion's paws and head

The god with the physiognomy of an old man is probably Uranus, who is the personification of the heavens and the father of the Titans. At the left is his daughter Themis, a goddess of law and justice.

At the left is the Titan, Phoebe (the radiant one), with a torch and her daughter, Asteria (the starry one), with a sword accompanied by a dog. In the frieze, they lead the gods of the morning and evening star

SOUTHERN PROJECTING HALL
BESIDE THE
GREAT STAIRWAY

Three nymphs, the female nature demons, are from Dionysus's entourage. On the cornice is the name of the artist, Theorretos

Dionysus, the god of vegetation, fertility and wine, is accompanied here by two boyish satyrs and his mother, Semele, who leads a lion into the battle

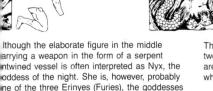

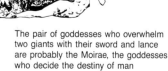

Although the elaborate figure in the middle carrying a weapon in the form of a serpent entwined vessel is often interpreted as Nyx, the goddess of the night. She is, however, probably one of the three Erinyes (Furies), the goddesses of revenge who punish evil doers

The pair of goddesses who overwhelm two giants with their sword and lance are probably the Moirae, the goddesses who decide the destiny of man

The lion goddess is generally recognized as Keto, the mother of the Graiae who would have followed at the left. She gave birth to terrible monsters like the fish (Ketos, Greek: whale, 'cetacean') at the left of her feet

The god of the sea, Poseidon, rises from his watery domain with a fantastic team of seahorses

23

animals and figures of gods and numerous sculptures once stood in the altar area. This extensive artistic program is filled with references to Pergamon's political history. The artistic imagery varies constantly, reflecting its function and placement on the building. The relief figures, worked almost in the round, seem to jostle one another for space and due to their large size, seem to strain the boundaries of the architectural framework. In contrast, the Telephus frieze is articulated and organized like an epic and its scenes depicting nature and interior spaces are calm and controlled very different from those in the Great Frieze.

The figures of gods set on the roof were sculpted to be viewed from below and are therefore only summarily worked on their backs. The Great Frieze with more than one hundred over lifesize figures surrounding the altar is of the highest artistic quality. Almost every scene in this battle between the gods and the giants is filled with dramatic tension and churning movement. A number of the goddesses have also joined in and even if they seldom physically overcome their enemies, their dominance is evident as they observe their opponents with cool, thoughtful superiority. In contrast, and often with merciless realism, the spiritual torment, pain and relentless cruelty of their extermination is reflected in the faces and bodies of the giants. No group is like the other and the differences in clothing and hair, even footwear, are elaborated down to the smallest detail. It must have been an artist of exceptional artistic creativity who conceived this extraordinary frieze. A group of experienced master sculptors and builders, as well as a group of artisans responsible for the detail work, must have been needed to bring the master plan to reality.

Unfortunately, the name of the artist who designed the Great Frieze is not preserved. A single inscription on the frieze naming the artist Theorretos can be assigned to its original place at the southern side of the steps. The preserved names of other artists who worked on the altar show that they came from the leading artistic centers of the Hellenistic world to work on the altar at Pergamon. We can be sure that the head artist was assisted by scholars, priests and members of the royal house while designing the thematic and compositional structure of this unusually long frieze.

The battle of the gods and giants was a popular theme in Greek art. For each Athenian festival, a new representation of the battle of the gods and the giants was woven into the fabric cloak for the cult statue of Athena Parthenos. In addition, specific scenes from the battle were represented in the fourteen metopes of the Parthenon in Athens. The battle of the gods and giants became a symbol of the Attic State. It commemorated the Athenians' victory over the Persians and was a visual expression of the victory of the Athenians over their enemies. Surely this thought also played a role at Pergamon. As the Athenians had done before them, the Pergamenians erected a commemorative monument decorated with the battle of the gods and giants which symbolized their victory over the enemies of Pergamon.

The similarity between the two events was also reiterated at the Athenian Acropolis where the kings of Pergamon dedicated statue groups depicting the demise of their mythological and historical enemies. The Persians appear as Amazons and the Gauls as giants. Such representations also clearly conceal a rulership ideology which saw the myth as a negative confrontation between divine order and barbarianism to be interpreted not only to their own advantage but also to be used for their own propagandistic ends. Their victory was the victory of order over chaos.

The sheer length of the relief, 120 meters, made it necessary to redesign the battle of the gods and the giants whereby older traditions, such as Hesiod's *Theogony* (Creation of the Gods), and Homer's epics were taken into consideration. Moreover, contemporary Hellenic epics and poetry surely provided additional stimuli. The myth relates the story of the earth mother Gaia who, from the blood of the emasculated Uranos, gave birth to the sons of the earth who would overthrow the Olympian Dynasty. An oracle had predicted that the gods would only be able to resist the giants when a mortal could be won over to participate in the battle. The part fell to the Greek hero Herakles who fights at the side of the father of the gods, Zeus, in the Great Frieze. Herakles's prominent position in the frieze demonstrates his special connection to the Royal House of Pergamon. The Attalids considered themselves direct descendants of Herakles's son Telephus whose life and accomplishments, including the founding of the city of Pergamon and the dedication of its sanctuary, are depicted in the small frieze set in the walls surrounding the altar for burnt offerings. Like Theseus in Athens, Telephus was an important local hero and the kings of Pergamon, as his heirs, emphasized this special connection.

Despite its fragmentary condition, the exceptional artistic importance of the Great Frieze can not be overlooked. It integrates the knowledge of generations of sculptors and at the same time continues the tradition. Each group of figures in the Great Frieze is worked with the viewpoint of the observer in mind whereby foreshortening and shifted perspective are calculated to perfection.

The sculpting of the scenes is a wonder in refinement; the sweeping folds of the garments and most of the weapons represented in stone are cut deep into the background leaving only fragile bridges of marble. Other materials, like

Fig. 17
The giant Alkyoneus,
Athena's opponent

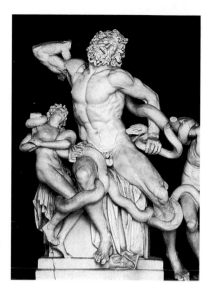

Fig. 18
The Laokoon Group
Roman copy of a
Pergamene original of
about 150–140 BC
Museo Vaticano, Rome
(Photograph: Bernard
Andreae)

the bronze and gold which must have been used for the jewelry of the goddesses, are not preserved. Even the paint which once covered the bluish marble is lost.

THE GREAT FRIEZE

THE EASTERN FRIEZE OF THE ALTAR

The representation of the dramatic struggle between the gods and the giants should not be interpreted as a series of events, but rather a single moment, exploding in simultaneous action and culminating in the battle's climax.
Entering the altar terrace from the street, the ancient visitor approached the back of the altar and its eastern frieze oriented toward the rising sun. Here a battle has erupted involving primarily the Olympian gods. Through the middle of the eastern frieze Hera drives the four powerful steeds of Zeus, throwing numerous giants to the ground. Not a single giant is able to hold his ground against these magnificent winged horses. The action leads on in the direction of the central group with Zeus and his daughter, Athena. To the left of the figure of Zeus we can probably reconstruct Herakles's mighty form. To Athena's right the war god, Ares, drives his team into battle.
The Zeus and Athena group is a remarkable composition. Their forms worked parallel to the relief ground are actually bound together by just the movements which appear to pull them apart. The composition is clearly

related to another famous work of art in the western gable of the Parthenon on the Acropolis of Athens, the struggle between Athena and Poseidon. Other references to early works of art also appear in the eastern frieze of The Pergamon Altar like the youthful figure of the god Apollo in the left section of the frieze. Here embodying the current ideal of beauty, he is in the act of removing an arrow from his quiver. The figure recalls the Classical Apollo form, the best known being the famous Apollo Belvedere whose original was probably created by the sculptor Leochares around 330 BC. The target of one of Apollo's arrows, a youthful giant sinks to the ground at Apollo's feet. In this case, one is reminded of the mythological giant Ephialtes who collapses with his eye pierced by an arrow.
Apollo is at the head of a family of Olympian gods. Apollo's mother, Leto, fights at his side and is followed by his sister, the goddess of the hunt, Artemis. At the end of the frieze the triple-bodied goddess Hekate, a daughter of Asteria, is drawn into the battle. Not far away in the southern frieze, she and her mother battle the giants.
Throughout the frieze the designer used genealogical, compositional and iconographical references, even drawing the frieze's narrative around its corners to show that the battle between the gods and giants as a sequence and not just a series of separate events. For example, in the southern frieze a giant sinks to ground at the feet of Phoebe's opponent, the victim of Cybele's arrow. This young, serpent-legged giant falls forward and, like Ephialtes, clutches the deadly arrow which has pierced his breast instead of his eye.

Eastern Frieze

HEKATE

ARTEMIS

◁ *Fig. 19*
Hekate and Artemis with their
opponents

Fig. 20 Eastern Frieze
Leto in battle with Tityos and
Apollo

LETO

APOLLON

Fig. 21 Eastern Frieze
Zeus fighting the giants

ZEUS

30

Fig. 22 Eastern Frieze
Athena fighting the giants

Fig. 23 Southern Frieze
Rhea/Cybele and three other gods fighting against a bull-neck giant

▷

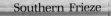

RHEA

Southern Frieze

EOS

Southern Frieze

HELIOS

Fig. 25
Two gods on the Southern Frieze

◁ *Fig. 24*
Helios with his team of horses

THE SOUTHERN FRIEZE OF THE ALTAR

The Titans, Phoebe (the radiant one) and her daughter, Asteria (the starry one), lead us to the deities of light and daytime on the southern frieze. Although major central sections of the frieze are missing, the primary gods of the daytime may be identified. In the left half of the frieze they are led by Eos, the goddess of the dawn who races into the fray on her horse. She is followed by the sun god, Helios, who rises out of the sea in his quadriga; even the giant who attempts to stand in the way of the chariot can not hinder him. Turned away from the viewer, the moon goddess,

PHOIBE

ASTERIA

KPIH

Selene, rides her mule across the body of one of the dead giants.

The central theme here is the advance of time which not even the intervention of the giants can arrest. In the last third of the southern frieze the gods intervene in the battle, led by the commanding presence of a goddess mounted on a lion. She is the mother of the gods, Rhea-Cybele, a goddess who was particularly revered in Asia Minor. An unusually dense group of figures is clustered around a muscular, steer-necked giant who is struck by a naked god with arms raised. Not alone, he is assisted by a goddess who appears in front of Rhea-Cybele and to the right, before the steer-necked giant, another god thrusts his weapon into the breast of the giant.

Fig. 26
The Titans, Phoebe and her daughter Asteria (the starry one)

37

Fig. 27
Triton and Amphitrite

Fig. 28
Sea gods on the northern side of the great stairway

THE SOUTHERN AND NORTHERN PROJECTING HALLS AT THE WEST SIDE OF THE ALTAR

In the section of frieze at the end of the southern projecting hall, Dionysus fights at the side of his mother, Semele, who was one of Zeus's lovers. Here again, a lion appears to help Semele in the battle. Dionysus is accompanied by two young satyrs and a panther whose representation is now almost completely lost. At the sides of the steps next to

Dionysus are three goddesses who are probably nymphs from the god's entourage.

Three pairs of sea gods dominate the battle on the altar's northern projecting hall; at the side of the stairs, Doris and Nereus, Okeanos and Tethys and on the end of the hall, Amphitrite and her son Triton. Their natural element, the sea, is omnipresent. The gods' wet garments cling to their bodies or sag in heavy folds. Nereus wears a fish skin on his head and Doris's shoes are made of fish skin and fins. Triton is particularly fanciful as the embodiment of this natural force. He is represented with the massive body of a fish complete with fins, the forelegs of a horse and widespread wings constructed of leaves which all lend to his impressive image. His body no longer touches the surface of the earth as he fights the giants who have sunk to their knees. While one giant is lacerated by Triton's hooves, the other is squashed by the god's massive fish body. With his sword, Triton tears away the lion skin meant to protect a third giant who is storming in his direction.

Fig. 29
A goddess on the Northern Frieze

THE NORTHERN FRIEZE OF THE ALTAR

Some of the gods that we have already encountered in the western and eastern frieze also join in the battle on the northern frieze and reinforce the genealogical relationships of the battle participants. The goddess, Aphrodite, and her mother, Dione, from Ares's entourage in the eastern frieze, add their support to the death dealing war god and thus survive the battle in their own way. Aphrodite tears a lance from the breast of a dead giant and Dione, flanked by Eros, fights a snake-legged giant.

In contrast, on the right side of the frieze, beginning at the corner of the projecting hall, the sea gods continue the family battle. Unfortunately, Poseidon's once magnificent team of seahorses surrounded by fish is mostly destroyed. Similar to the scene with Helios's team, a giant also stood in the way.

The names of the numerous goddesses in the right section of the north frieze and of the gods in the left central part of the northern frieze are still not certain. From the inscriptions on the ledges we know that Graiae, Moirae (Fates) and Erinyes (Furies) were probably present in the right half of the frieze. They are preceded by the superb form of a youthful goddess who enters the fray with a vase wound round with serpents like those used as weapons in the war between Rome and Carthage. Filled with poisonous snakes, this vessel and other weapons like the Macedonian shield in front of Hera's quadriga symbolize the historical enemies of Pergamon.

The left half of the frieze is filled with a dense group of fighting gods who have not yet been completely identified. The so-called biter group, in which a giant grabs a god and raises him over his head while digging his teeth into the god's upper arm, is so unusual that it deserves special mention. The god, locked in the giant's clutches, will have his difficulties extracting himself from this desperate situation. Perhaps this is Castor whose brother, Polydeuces, hurries to his assistance from the left.

Fig. 30
The goddess Aphrodite

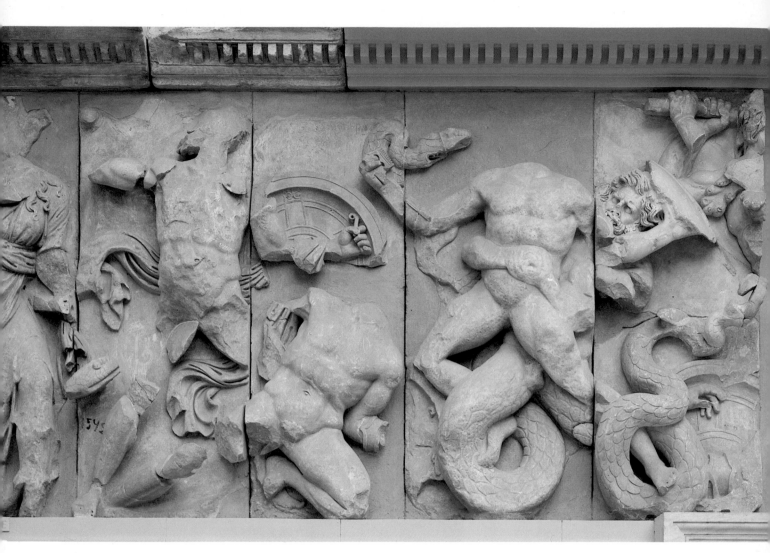

Fig. 31
The so-called biter group

Fig. 32   ▷
A goddess, perhaps one of the Erinys

Fig. 34
Herakles finds his son, Telephus

◁ Fig. 33
The building of Auge's boat

THE TELEPHUS FRIEZE

The altar for burnt offerings stood in the middle of the court of the Great Altar. The walls of this court were decorated with a small frieze, 1.58 meter high. Although such interior spaces were usually covered with paintings, here we find a wonderful relief sequence whose story unfolds like a picture book transformed into stone. After the court's enclosure wall was erected, the scenes were carved right into the stone.

In contrast to the Great Frieze which captures a tension filled moment in the mythological battle between the giants and gods, the small frieze narrates the life and deeds of Telephus, the city's founding father. Telephus, a son of Herakles and legendary founder of the cult of Pergamon, was revered by the kings of Pergamon as their ancestor and they drew their legitimacy as rulers from his mythological deeds and his role as founder of the kingdom of Pergamon. The inhabitants of Pergamon saw themselves as "Telephidai", descendants of Telephus. The contemporary significance of the myth was part of a carefully structured propaganda program directed at the ancient observers to emphasize the similarity between mythological events and their own history. Further, because they were subject to the accidents of fate, the depicted episodes from Telephus's life were intended to serve as a role model.

Although there were several versions of the legend, contemporary Hellenistic mythologists may well have expanded the story to make the Pergamon version more interesting to its viewers.

The Telephus legend depicted in the interior court is also related to the epic struggle of the gods and giants in the Great Frieze. The Greek hero, Herakles, is not only the decisive factor in the battle against the giants, but as the father of the founder of the city, Telephus is the link between the two friezes. In the large frieze, Herakles fights beside his father Zeus and in the small frieze he appears himself in the role of father and savior of Telephus.

With the help of ancient versions of the story and relief remains, the following story outline may be reconstructed. The oracle of Apollo of Delphi warned King Aleos of Arcadia that his daughter's descendants would bring him harm. To avert danger he donates his daughter, Auge, to the goddess Athena as a priestess. While Herakles is staying at King Aleos's court he meets Auge and a clandestine affair between the pair produces a son whose name is Telephus. To forestall the prophesied evil, Aleos disowns his daughter and sets her adrift in a sealed boat. The construction of this boat is depicted on two of the relief panels (fig. 33). King Aleos stands at the left and personally supervises the

Fig. 35
Companions of Telephus

Fig. 36
Teuthras and Auge

construction of the boat by four men working with hand tools. Wrapped in a cloak drawn over her head, Auge sadly sits on a rock above the scene. Similar to Classical grave reliefs, her grief is symbolized by the gesture of the hand held to the chin. Two servants stand before her with an open casket. Auge's boat eventually reaches the coast of Mysia in Asia Minor where she is welcomed by King Teuthras and his attendants. The myth and the frieze further relates how Teuthras took Auge as his daughter and how Auge, in thanks for her deliverance and the kind reception, founded the cult of Athena in Mysia.

Faced with the problem of what to do with Auge's baby son, King Aleos abandons him just after birth in the plane tree grove of the sanctuary. As one of the reliefs reveals, it is in

this very grove that Herakles is later united with his infant son (fig. 34). Casually Herakles leans on his massive club, draped with a lion skin. His glance rests on the lioness at his feet suckling the child Telephus. The idyllic setting is depicted with great care and includes many details like the gnarled plane tree with branches and leaves carved at the left edge of the relief, the high cliff at the right side and the lioness who lies at the entrance of the cave, all of which enhance the pictorial quality of the narrative.

Having attained manhood, Telephus fulfils the oracle's terrible prophecy and slays his mother's brothers. Recognized by Aleos, he is laden with curses and leaves the country. Finally he arrives at the court of Teuthras in Mysia where he is warmly welcomed and bidden by the king to

46

help fight the enemies of Mysia. As a reward he will be made king of Mysia and Auge will be his consort. When the victorious Telephus returns from his mission he becomes king of Mysia. During his wedding to Auge, however, the serpent sacred to Athena reveals the true identity of the pair as mother and son. The following scenes tell of Telephus's deeds as king of Mysia. Amongst other things, the Greeks invade his land and during the ensuing battles his wife, the Amazon Hiera, is killed.

Telephus is also wounded. While fighting with Achilles he gets caught in the tendrils of a grapevine which the wrathful Dionysus had cultivated and wounds his leg on Achilles's lance. An oracle has prophesied that only the cause of the wound can heal it. Telephus, therefore, goes to Argos and asks to be healed. The welcome and the ceremonial banquet prepared for his reception are partially preserved in the fragmentary panels. The architectural device of two columns suggests an interior space where five men sit together on stools enjoying the feast.

Two servants, a cup bearer who serves the wine and a boy with the dish of fruit, frame the scene. The bearded man at the right represents Telephus as he gathers back his cloak and exposes the wound on his thig, thereby revealing his identity. The legend reveals how Agamemnon hesitated to help Telephus and how Telephus in his distress seized the king's little son, Orestes, and threatened to kill him on the house altar. Thanks to a tip from Odysseus, however, Telephus learns that it is not Achilles, but his spear that can heal the wound. In gratitude, Telephus leads the Greeks to victory over Troy and upon his return founds Pergamon and its cult centers.

Unlike the Great Frieze, the few preserved sections of the Telephus Frieze are smaller, the relief is lower and they are carved in a very different style. We know from the construction of The Pergamon Altar that the Telephus frieze was carved a bit later than the Great Frieze. Its style, however, is not a reflection of its date. Its epical story sequence and its proximity to the observer have necessitated a new style. We see landscapes of almost idyllic character and architectural elements that suggest interiors. The staggering of figures, of empty spaces above figure groups or figures and of objects receding into space are also part of this new style. The result is a new spatial relationship in which the volume of the figures and their depth visually free the relief wall. The artistic innovations of the Telephus Frieze proved unusually influential and served as a catalyst for the artistic reforms of Late Hellenistic and Roman relief style.

Fig. 37 ▷
View from the Acropolis of Pergamon (Photograph: Max Kunze)

Model of the Pergamon Acropolis
(cf. fig. 10, p. 15)

1   Storage magazines
2   Palace I
3   Palace III
4   Palace IV
5   Palace V
6   Gate
7   Temple sanctuary of Athena
8   Trajaneum (temple built by the Roman
    emperor Trajan)
9   Library
10 Theater of Dionysus
11 Temple of Dionysus
12 The Pergamon Altar
13 Upper Agora (marketplace)
14 Heroon (building for the celebration of
    the cult of the local rulers)